FROM THE BODY

From the Body

edited by
CHARLEY BARNES

Valley Press

First published in 2023 by Valley Press
Woodend, The Crescent, Scarborough, YO11 2PW
www.valleypressuk.com

ISBN 978-1-915606-09-9
Cat. no. VP0216

Editorial copyright © Charley Barnes 2023
Individual copyright © as credited 2023

The right of the individuals to be identified as the
authors of these works has been asserted in accordance
with the Copyright, Designs and Patents Act 1988.

All rights reserved. No part of this publication may be
reproduced, stored in or introduced into a retrieval system,
or transmitted in any form, by any means (electronic,
mechanical, photocopying, recording or otherwise) without
prior written permission from the rights holders.

A CIP record for this book is available from the British Library.

Cover and text design by Peter Barnfather.
'Still Life with Flowers and a Watch' by Abraham Mignon, c. 1660–1679,
collection of the Rijksmuseum, Dupper Wzn. Bequest, Dordrecht.
Edited by Charley Barnes.

Printed and bound in Great Britain
by Imprint Digital, Upton Pyne, Exeter.

Contents

Foreword • *Charley Barnes* 11

Kefir • *Wendy Allen* 15
The day you meet hunger is the day you will suffer • *Faye Alexandra Rose* 16
From Corner Shop to Comment Section • *Jaimi Shrive* 19
Contingency plans and plastic pipes • *Kayla Jenkins* 24
Reflections On Henry Ford Hospital or Three Men in A Room Dissecting My Period • *Cassie Evelyn Johnson* 28
Doctors, Please, Be More Individual • *Donna M Day* 32
Never too much and always enough • *Cara Lisette* 37
Towards a Kingless Kingdom • *Clare Fisher* 44
The Gadget • *Ade Couper* 49
Digging for the Bones • *Rue Collinge* 53
My Body, My Captor • *Abbie Rutherford* 59

An authentic portrait of my family's meals
  • *Clare Law*   62
Tangled • *Val Fraser*   68
From the Belly • *Andrew McMillan*   72
Never Been Quite Right • *T.G. Hofman*   75
Finding my Skin • *Daisy Black*   78

Contributors   83
Acknowledgements   89

Foreword

I am not the type of person to develop an eating disorder.

This is a sentence I have said more times than I can remember. But I still don't know what I mean when I say it: not about the 'type' of person I perceive to be susceptible to this family of mental illnesses, nor about myself. Though the pandemic has taught me that much of what I knew about both is more changeable than I first realised. *From the Body* is an extension of this. What I thought I knew about this book when I first drafted an outline for it was wrong; though perhaps not wrong entirely, it was certainly changeable. It wasn't until the essays began to arrive in the inbox that I realised, though I suppose not for the first time, our bodies and how we fuel them are topics tender to the touch – with different bruising, different hypersensitivities, and different comfort zones.

In collating these essays, though, I have seen a commendable amount of bravery from the contributing authors who word by word have dismantled their comfort. *From the Body* is built from lived and now shared experiences; lived by people who have struggled and healed – or even, people who are still healing. In many ways, I think most of us have something to heal from in terms of our physical form. The degrees to which these things – these experiences we survived, or these things about our bodies we might not like – the way they affect us may vary. Still, there is something about the body for the majority of us.

From a young age I struggled with my own – from being in a wheelchair, to gaining weight, losing weight and then, recently, losing more. Throughout those states I don't know that I've ever been comfortable, or even especially kind, to the bones and muscle that house me. Spirited by the contributing authors here, I feel brave enough to admit there are times when I've been decidedly unkind if anything. If a friend spoke to me how I've spoken to my body, I'd be moved to swiftly show them the door. Though I have learned I'm far from the only person to have a sometimes toxic relationship with myself. Similarly, I'm not the only person looking to heal from that. In many ways, though, *From the Body* was a selfish endeavour to begin with. I wanted to know more about the available narratives that exist around our physical forms – and my, don't I know more now. Not everything, I hasten to add, but certainly more.

Lest the opportunity pass me by, then, I'd like to thank all the authors who submitted work to this project – not only those who were accepted. In opening that inbox, there came a flurry of narratives dealing in disability, gender representation, mental illness, patriarchy, parental influences, the media and more. These topics, alongside others, are housed in this final form of the book, and I hope that they will bring you comfort and outrage and kinship.

The essays have been given Content Warnings where appropriate, so please do take note of these and be gentle with your selves when reading. These works aren't always soft-edged – but the most important things seldom are.

Reader, whatever your reasons for coming to this book, I hope you take something away.

Warmest, Charley

Kefir

Wendy Allen

1. I am told to drink bacteria to help my gut, this will stop me being so fucked up.

2. I cannot survive without it.

3. I am led to believe my body is cruel, yet this will make me hungry again –

4. I think of peaches, tomatoes, I think of raspberries. I think of my lover.

5. My lover says my lips taste sour, a baby's bubbled breath, off milk.

6. I curdle under liquid which is blanket heavy.

7. I taste of drowning.

8. At sea, at sea, at sea.

9. I am sick, acid fragranced, drip-fed badness.

The day you meet hunger is the day you will suffer

Faye Alexandra Rose

cw. Restrictive eating behaviours, disordered eating, sexual assault

I often took nourishment for granted. I placed food into my mouth and chewed, a mundane task to keep myself fuelled for daily routines. 'Calories' was merely a word I saw printed on magazines and inside the slimming world leaflets that were posted through my mother's letterbox. I had no use for it in my vocabulary. My relationship with food was healthy, until the moment my body became a stranger.

I remember the exact moment food became ammunition to inflict pain upon myself. It was moments after I was left on the floor of a hotel room in the middle of the night. I crawled to the bathroom and switched on the light, and I was confronted with the night's events written all over my skin. I remember looking at her, someone with a distant haze of familiarity, yet so unknown. I became so consumed with disgust and anguish for my own body that mirrors became a place for ridicule and resentment. The months that followed that night were filled with police investigations and examinations. Strangers looking at my body with a question mark; more strangers questioning my truth when the grief was seeping out of my pores. My body – a home once filled with love – became barren.

When the body is deserted, there is nothing left to sustain. I was left with a shell that I felt wasn't worthy of nourishment. Food went from something I enjoyed to something I both feared and relished in rejecting. I was a walking paradox; I wanted to maintain a level of pain that I had become accustomed to, whilst attempting to gain any resemblance of control and reason over my own body. Food became the only thing I had a choice over in my life during that time and it became so interwoven with my grief that I couldn't tell the difference between self-destruction and healing. This period was made harder to navigate as I received compliments from those around me. 'I wish I had your body,' was something I heard almost daily. 'No, you don't!' I would scream internally. 'My body isn't my own anymore!' Whilst replying with a nod and a slight resemblance of a smile. I was left feeling baffled at how the visible representation of my suffering became so desirable to others, and how restricting my food intake could lead to such a magnitude of compliments.

I started to rattle I was so thin. Clothing began to hang off my body like a coat hanger – no soft edges filled with stories of a life enjoyed, just someone that wanted to hide from the world. My mother watched her daughter disappear in front of her eyes, desperately cooking favourite dishes in attempt to spark a remanence of normality back into my mind. Every day she would place them in front of me at the dinner table. 'Remember?' Her eyes always spoke more than her mouth ever could. I would often fall to my knees from the hunger pains, curling into the foetal position on my bedroom floor, screaming for it to all go away. But once dispersed I would always find myself back in front of the mirror picking once more at my faults. I remember one evening I kneaded the small pouch left remaining on my stomach and sobbed at my failure for having not removed it. I was convinced that removing that would make my life go back to normal, how it was before.

The next day I received a phone call from the police explaining that the investigation into the incident was being dropped due to 'insufficient evidence' and from that moment on my health went from bad to worse. I was going days without adequate food. Life and my future became bleak, and I started to reason that if I didn't act, I may not survive this illness.

One evening in May 2018, after a particularly exhausting breakdown in front of the mirror, I researched counselling for eating disorders in my local area. I filled out the form, took a deep breath and pressed send. Days later I received a phone call. 'It's not your fault,' the woman reassured me, 'I promise one day you will be okay again.' The kind distant words of optimism that years later became my reality.

I know now that food became a coping mechanism. During that period of my life, my body represented an end goal; not death, not perfection, not even the desperation to be 'thin', but to make my feelings somehow tangible. I was so desperate to feel anything, even starvation, rather than to be consumed with the feeling of his hands on my skin. Focusing on food allowed my mind to be distracted from my reality, allowing the festering problems to be pushed to the side lines. It was during these desperate moments of my life that I realised how mental and physical health are inescapable from one another, and how food is not only nourishment for the body, but for the mind.

From Corner Shop to Comment Section

Jaimi Shrive

'STARS LOSE FIGHT WITH CELLULITE'

'SKINNY, BONY & HAGGARD'

'50 WORST BEACH BODIES'

As a child and in my very early teen years, I saw the models on the covers of magazines, and celebrated in the media, and I recognised how similar my own body was to theirs. It made me feel proud. Looking back, I internalised these messages to such an extent that I even felt somewhat critical of other girls who didn't have the same body, which had been sold to us all as 'healthy', 'beautiful', and worryingly 'sexy' (I'll revisit this later). I didn't understand how other girls must be living when I could attend just one sports club each week and even manage to sneak extra junk food out of the treat cupboard, and still have such a 'healthy' body. They must have been *really* unhealthy, I assumed, and I promised myself I'd always keep my body exactly the way it was. Of course, this was next to impossible.

I'd already begun to internalise the patriarchy's expectations of women's bodies…

There are three things you can always guarantee while

browsing through the corner shop's magazine section: body shaming, diet culture, and adverts for the latest miracle products to change your appearance. The three statements at the top of this piece are all headline quotes from UK magazines. Such magazines notoriously target a female audience, while simultaneously shaming women's appearances. These messages are both fed by and accepted into the patriarchal society we live in. This is probably the reason I took on such complex messages about body image; both my own, and how women and girls should look.

I remember as a young teen fixating myself on ensuring my legs never got any bigger. I'd avoid exercise that contributed to muscle growth because I'd decided I couldn't afford for them to get any larger. They were already the same size as some models I'd see on the cover of these magazines in corner shops, and I still hadn't finished growing. Then, as my body started to go through more stages of puberty, I would run at 6:00 am before school each morning, and by then my appetite had shrunk dramatically too. I thought about what my slightly younger self believed a healthy body looked like and I felt an obligation to not let her down. With hindsight, I was probably already a manifestation of society's attitudes towards women's bodies, even as my younger self.

As I've got older (I'm soon to be 24), it's dawned on me that my childhood body was exactly that: the body of a *child*. It's only over the last twelve months that I have contemplated the gravity of my stress at growing into a woman, and losing the body type that society not only holds up as one of health, but also sexualises – and 'sexy' women wouldn't be subjected to scrutiny... or so I thought.

The pressure on women to retain their 'schoolgirl figure' is a very sinister one which is held up in all forms of media, and it was evidently powerful enough to influence me, even as a twelve-year-old.

In fact, it was during a recent period of great stress in my life, when my clothing size dramatically dropped, that I got the most compliments on my body I've ever had. People would tell me that I looked 'really well' and women would tell me, 'I wish my figure still looked like that!' Honestly, I too thought I looked great. In reality though, I was anything but healthy. I was anything but healthy. So the lie that being thin automatically means being healthy unravelled in my mind, completely.

Fitness and fashion models have always been held as the pinnacle of health, and the thinner they got, the healthier and fitter they must be. All weight loss is applauded, no matter how much, for what reason, in what context or how fast. Where were the articles talking about the impact of thinness? The articles that were clearly arguing that thin didn't mean healthy?

When I was at my thinnest, I often complained about my hair falling out in handfuls and my skin being bad. I never considered that it was connected to my weight, because I was slim, so I was healthy. Right?

Alongside the turbulence of my weight, I also spent years not sleeping. If I went to bed around 10:00 pm, I wouldn't be able to drop off until 2:00 am, would then sleep for 2-3 hours, before waking up again at 5:00 am and not being able to rest. I spent years falling asleep again by 11:00 am, and then again at 3:00 pm. At the time, I thought those severe fluctuations in my energy levels were normal.

It's been a complex and slow process, challenging years of deliberate, societal grooming which left me with two opposing, hypocritical views about body image and weight. On the one hand, I believed that people come in all different shapes and sizes and that this is ok and should be celebrated. On the other hand, I believed my perceived worth in society was dictated by the way my body looked.

While some of these magazines that body shame women and encourage diet supplements are facing more scrutiny than ever before, something much more impactful is targeting the next generation of young girls. Girls just like I was, browsing front covers of 'women's mags' and examining themselves through every angle in the mirror, are today navigating the endless adverts of 'weight-loss coffee', 'detox tablets' and cosmetic surgery, alongside constant and inescapable criticism of women's bodies on countless social media posts. I realised, after years of something in the back of my mind ticking away, that women's bodies, no matter their size and shape, will *always* be scrutinised as if we're public property.

The quotes below were some of the top most 'liked' comments from the comment section of three different articles written about women that had been shared to my feed in one day:

'Anyone who says she's beautiful is just a liar'

'Real women have a bit of meat on their bones!'

'Women of her size shouldn't be featured, it's encouraging obesity!'

'She looks like a blowup sex doll'

The narratives surrounding women's bodies and weight are much like the ones I was fed as a child and teenager: contradictory. It appears impossible for women to exist at any size, structure, or shape without being shamed or criticised. There is immense flexibility in the social narratives, meaning that virtually any body type can be simultaneously celebrated and hated at any given moment. Despite this, in yet another dichotomy, in which all female body types are subjected to scrutiny, the ideal slim female body still reigns supreme. Whilst some may argue that 'skinny-shaming' exists, there is no evidence to suggest that it has anywhere near the power of 'fat-shaming'. This in itself lends support to the powerful social messages given to me, and billions of other women and girls, that thin equals good, and fat equals bad.

Our insecurity then, of whether we are good or bad, thin or fat, attractive or ugly, wanted or unwanted, is relentlessly and successfully exploited and capitalised upon by corporations and industries. In everything from food to fashion, it pays to keep women and girls feeling ashamed, scared, and under pressure to conform to desirability and femininity.

And perhaps the biggest and most powerful industry of all ultimately achieves all its core aims by keeping women and girls busy worrying about how much the numbers on the scales have moved, and what size their jeans are. The patriarchy is able to tie women and girls up in knots as they attempt to reach an unreachable ideal, whilst simultaneously attacking other women for also not reaching a patriarchal ideal.

Contingency plans and plastic pipes

Kayla Jenkins

cw: Disordered eating, health anxiety

It began inconspicuously enough. I'd enjoyed too much of a housemate's food during her turn of our university flat's own *Come Dine With Me* and spent the rest of the night lying on my side in bed with a bin in the predicted splash zone. Such a sin, I know, but not an uncommon act for a university student. In my head I made contingency plans: What would my path to the toilet be? What if I got it on the duvet? What if I wake up any of the others?

I wasn't sick that night, but I still woke up the next morning with caution. I ate bland toast for breakfast, something my mum always told me would help settle the stomach. When it came to tea time, I had a plain bowl of pasta and tried to ignore the nagging fear that it would again make me feel sick. It did.

Every meal thereafter, I felt sick to some degree. The weight began to drop off me like overcooked meat on the bone, only eating half a meal here and half a meal there. Sometimes, it took only half a slice of toast to set me off. Not even the thickest, butteriest crust could entice me to push through despite the nausea rising.

After a couple of weeks, I finally booked in to see the GP. They initially chalked it down to stress, told me to come back a week later if it persisted. A week later I was back, and so the investigations began. The abdomen pressing – 'Sorry about my choice of knickers… does it hurt there? Or here?' – the elimination dieting to rule out being lactose intolerant, or celiac; the blood tests, the urine samples, the stool samples, the ultrasounds, the sedation-free gastroscopy. I was left choking on a plastic pipe while a nurse stroked my hair and coached me 'just thirty seconds more'. The only thing that didn't come my way were answers. Four years on and the latest ruling is a tentative note: SIGNIFICANT: Gastroesophageal reflux disease.

At one point, I fell so deep into the pit of recurrent nausea and stomach pain that other aspects of my life began to suffer. I no longer ate out at restaurants as I was too consumed with the worry of throwing up in a public bathroom. I became panicky on trains because I was scared of the toilet door whirring open to reveal me on the bathroom floor, head in the bowl, retching to high hell and back. A pitiful *Take Me Out* entrance where all the travellers would buzz their red lights the second they saw me. I'd never make it further than Preston before getting off and getting right back on the next train home to Blackpool North, tearfully making phone calls of apology in the meantime.

I can't pinpoint exactly when the paranoia began to set in even more insistently. I stopped eating certain foods in case they weren't cooked properly. I obsessively checked the dates of foods, and wouldn't eat anything nearing a sell-by – yet another reason why I wouldn't eat anything I couldn't personally check over beforehand. I became suspicious. I stopped eating out with friends because I was scared they'd notice me skirting around the plate, fork and food in some unwinnable stand-off. It was frustrating because, my god, I love to eat, and I've been a serial snacker for as long as I can remember. But now, every piece of food was becoming a threat to me and I eyed it with tired eyes.

I think it was during my third year of uni that I started to wonder if it was beyond something physical. I'd noticed that I felt sick the more I thought about it, and the more I obsessed over it the worse it got. After a chat with the GP and a single therapy session on campus, I was put on Citalopram alongside my good ol' reliable Omeprazole. The term 'anxiety' began to be thrown around and I think, looking back now, anxiety is something I've always had. It shouldn't have surprised me when I began to think: What if we miss a serious problem because we've written it off simply as anxiety?

And so the panic set in again. I was terrified of dying in my sleep at twenty-three years old, becoming another tragic case of misdiagnoses or systemic failures. I felt guilty because I knew the healthcare professionals were trying, but I was tired of the testing and the uncertainty. Worse still, there were the derogatory comments made to me at work, things like, 'My dick is bigger than your waist.' At my lowest point, I was having panic attacks every day and only eating foods that were bland and often burnt to avoid being undercooked.

The problem still hasn't gone away now. Most of my friends don't know, at least not to the true extent, and it remains difficult even now to try and articulate in words what's gone on. Tests are ongoing to try and find the root of the issue; however, at this point, I've accepted it probably is at the very least aggravated by my anxieties. Whether it's an eating disorder or not is something that's been on my mind for a while now, but as of yet I've not been confident enough to confront that reality.

I'm back to eating more normally, though I still make a point to chew gum after every meal as I read once it helped with nausea. Sometimes I do wake up in the early hours of the morning with the incessant feeling of needing to gip, or with stomach cramps. Those are the times I've learnt to bring a blanket with me to the bathroom so afterwards I can sit at the living room window with the dog and a brew and watch the sun steadily rise. Some days are awful and often I have to come home early from an event as the all-too familiar feeling pits itself at the back of my throat. I still make contingency plans of what routes I'll take if I'm sick in the night, even if I never have been during the four years of whatever *this* is. The frustration of remaining undiagnosed, whichever way that diagnosis falls, is still there too. It'll take time, though. I know it will. As all things do.

Reflections On Henry Ford Hospital or Three Men in A Room Dissecting My Period

Cassie Evelyn Johnson

cw: Restrictive eating behaviours, disordered eating

The children's outpatient ward was not where I wanted to be that day. To have such a designation – *child* – attached to me made me acutely aware of the thing I was avoiding. But there I was, confronted with it: my infancy. The tininess of my body (although I didn't see it that way), the flatness of my chest. Diminutive, everywhere.

But some time before – a period I cannot remember exactly now, despite the way the event itself jutted into my memory, a memory which, I assume, has now been abstracted in some way – my body had signalled it was time to leave all that behind. And here I was, in a room with three men, ready to dissect that very thing.

First of all: my father. It really needn't have been my mother, and I wasn't concerned that it wasn't. But I suppose on that day in particular it might have been more appropriate. The second man: the consultant who had led my case since I'd been admitted. The one whose weight my mother always made comments about ('He's a doctor, he shouldn't be shaped like that.'). Even when I was beside her with a tube in my nose, being pushed every night closer to a size that I never wanted to be.

The third: a medical student. The consultant had checked beforehand that I was happy for him to be there. The idea that I, being as young and physically insignificant as I was, had the power to allow anyone to be anywhere was hilarious to me. But I didn't laugh, just quietly nodded. It was so much easier to be docile.

'She has some news,' my father said, and turned to me expectantly. 'My period started,' I told the consultant. As I said it my father lightly squeezed my arm and gave me a congratulatory smile that barely hid his relief. It was a sigh of a smile. I tried to smile back, but instead just looked away and found an unremarkable spot on the wall opposite to focus on so I wouldn't have to make eye contact with the consultant as he explained why this was such an important step.

I'd employed the same tactic years before, in one of my last meetings as an inpatient. They called them multidisciplinary meetings, supposedly the most useful, the most comprehensive. But I just felt that the more people there were in the room, the less I was in it. There was a medical student present on that day as well, and this time I'd chosen to stare at his shoes so that no one would be able to catch my eye and engage me. I hadn't said a word in at least five minutes. I was meant to have been discharged that week, but there had been a setback.

'She's lost weight,' one of the nurses said. And there I was, reduced to a number. 'She had a crying fit over an apple last week,' another nurse said. A behaviour. 'She told her roommate that she doubted whether recovery was even worth it.' An idea. It's so hard to remain personalised as you are medicalised.

And all I could think about in that moment was how much the medical student in the meeting looked like the grizzly one from Hot Chip. I began lightly tapping out the repetitive beat of one of their songs on the arm of my chair. Maybe they'd all think it was some kind of nervous tic. Maybe my grizzly student friend would make a note of it. But he spoke, and his words jolted me out of my daze. 'I think what Cassie's trying to say is....' And there it was, my voice again, spoken out the mouthpiece of another.

I returned to my spot on the wall of the children's outpatient ward. The consultant, now in the form of gatekeeper, told me that meant I was ready to be fully discharged. It didn't matter what was in my head, for my reproductive organs, the things that had once held me back, had set me free. I pictured that scene from *The Shining*: the elevator reaches ground with a chime, the doors grind open, blood spills out. I imagined that a scarlet-clad troop of dancers might follow me out of the ward, twirling red batons all the way to the carpark.

But that didn't happen. After all those years, after breaking myself, after months of hospitalisation, after hauling my weary limbs through recovery, my dad simply drove me back to school. 'We're so proud of you,' he said as I got out the car. I walked away. I couldn't help but feel I shouldn't be praised for something that was completely out of my hands, and merely a fulfilment of my binary-hugging, 'feminine' destiny anyway. A destiny which, in my eyes, would have been reached so much earlier and with greater ease had my mind not decided to attack my body.

Previously, when I thought of this moment, I would also think of *Henry Ford Hospital*: Frida Kahlo dissects elements of her reproductivity and suspends them around her. But still attached, with umbilical-like cords. Spectres, but ones that are a product of your existence. Ones ripe with sexist ideals of femininity to ensure you may never escape.

Henry Ford Hospital shows Kahlo recovering in hospital following a miscarriage. Some say she was ambivalent towards having kids. Others say that she resented the way her disability made it near impossible for her to bear children. We all put our own interpretations onto things. I used to look at this painting and feel kinship, feel that I understood. Obviously, I now see the ridiculous nature of this comparison. I see it all differently.

I see that life has given me the freedom of choice; has given me privilege. I see that now I can run my packs of Microgynon together and choose whether or not to have a period – the 7-day break was only invented to appease the Catholic church, after all. I see that not all women have periods and that not all those who have periods are women. That your ability to reproduce has no bearing on who you are as a person. And I also see that, no matter how well-functioning the body, the thing can always be lurking there, inside your head.

One more thing on interpretation – a few months after I was discharged as an outpatient, my parents went to a family party that I couldn't make. When a relative asked them how I was, my mother responded, 'Great actually, she started her period.' The family were aware of my illness, but I don't think the true weight of this news would have struck the relative in that moment; he was probably just left confused. I cringed when this anecdote was relayed to me later. My brother, of course, found it hilarious. But reflecting on it now, I think of my mother, ever the reserved stoic. And I think of the sheer relief that must have led her to make such an effusive disclosure. And I think that maybe these things do matter, just not for the reasons we are told they do.

Doctors, Please, Be More Individual

Donna M Day

Eating disorders are inextricably connected to weight. If you look up eating disorders, the first symptoms listed are around an obsession with or an effect on weight. If you ask someone about eating disorders often the first thing they will mention is weight. If people talk about their own eating disorders, they usually mention the effects on their weight first and foremost. Someone living with an eating disorder has a lot of symptoms, but the most visible symptoms, the symptoms that people can see, are the ones affecting their weight. But for me and my life with disordered eating, weight was very much a secondary consideration.

My later diagnosis of Obsessive Compulsive Disorder (OCD) led me to the conclusion that my eating disorder, which comprised various symptoms, was another set of compulsive behaviours. These behaviours were also far easier to integrate into my life than repeatedly checking my door was locked or unplugging everything in my house before leaving. After all, skipping breakfast could not make me late for work or leave me without hot water.

But the doctors who treated the eating disorder were focused on my weight, which did become dangerously low. They did not associate my eating disorder with my OCD. They associated it with my weight. And when my weight became satisfactory, they discharged me.

The symptoms of my eating disorder almost immediately recurred upon my discharge and remained at a dangerous level for many years. Today, the symptoms of my eating disorder, whom I affectionately refer to as Mia, loiter on the edges of my life, very rarely causing any major disruption though they are always there, whispering away.

And recently these whispers have become ever louder as Mia has crept closer and closer into daily life once more. Today, doctors are still obsessed with my weight, except this time I am on the wrong end of their colourful Body Mass Index (BMI) graph: I am officially obese.

Living with Polycystic Ovary Syndrome (PCOS) meant that shortly after my thirtieth birthday, my figure ballooned, seemingly overnight

Even though it is widely accepted and clinically proven that PCOS causes weight gain in and of itself, the universal cure offered by doctors everywhere is 'lose weight'. Losing weight apparently reduces the symptoms of PCOS, but as one of the symptoms of PCOS is itself weight gain, I'm at a loss to work out where one begins and the other ends.

Various other health conditions have left me disabled and exercise is therefore quite difficult. But my doctors insist that the best thing for my chronic pain as well as my PCOS is to lose weight.

For years, doctors told me to gain weight. My BMI was too low. I needed to hit a point on their graph. I was underweight, which was dangerous. My periods would stop. I wouldn't be able to have children. Now, doctors are telling to lose weight. My BMI is too high. I need to hit a point on the graph. I am in the orange section which means I am obese, which is dangerous. My periods might stop. I won't be able to have children.

One doctor actually said to me that if diet and exercise aren't working, maybe I should just stop eating altogether.

There it is. Mia's voice: 'I told you so. You are fat and disgusting and completely out of control. Just stop eating.'

And it would be so easy to do just that.

I diet. I exercise. My weigh-ins are reaching an obsessive level and it terrifies me. And it bewilders me that I can apparently gain considerable weight overnight. Every time I go to the doctors I am in the dangerous zone of their graphs and they don't believe me when I show them my own records, in the acceptable zone several times. The graph on my own records looks frighteningly like a mountain range.

Mia's voice is such a comfort through this. It would be so easy to surrender to her.

At the start of the pandemic, like so many others living with OCD, the calls from the government to constantly handwash, wipe surfaces, and not touch other people were like a licence for my compulsive behaviours. I had been proven right. You really should be using hand sanitiser whenever you touched something out in a public place. I was right all along.

And now, it seems, so is Mia.

My relationship with Mia is complicated and messy. She is still hanging around the edges of my life and I'm managing to not let her in and because of that I'm not eligible for any help. I'm not starving or purging, and most importantly of all, I am not remotely underweight. So, by definition, I do not have an eating disorder. I am recovered – apparently.

It doesn't matter what I say to the doctors about my behaviour or my thought patterns. The BMI graph says I am obese and therefore I am obese and I do not have an eating disorder.

The worst part of living by the BMI graph of course is that it's so widely discredited. You often hear stories of elite athletes being at the unhealthy end of the BMI graph, but outside of this anecdotal evidence is my own experience of medical professionals assessing my BMI.

I have recently had a Consultant Cardiologist tell me that it's absolute nonsense that I am obese, my weight is normal and healthy, and I do not need to lose the amount of weight I have been told I need to be a 'normal' weight. At another recent medical appointment, the nurse looked me up and down, laughed at the notion of my being obese and put me on the scales. Confused, she reviewed her colourful graph and said, 'Oh, yes, so you are… Well, the scales don't lie!' She told me to lose more weight and sent me home, backtracking on her earlier assertion that there was no way that I was obese.

Friends and family frown with concern when I tell them the magic number I have still to reach, telling me it's too far, I've lost enough weight and I would look ill.

Health is inextricably connected to weight. We live in a world obsessed with diets and weight loss where eating disorders are whispered about as a plague affecting teenaged girls caused by our obsession with diets and weight loss, and digitally altered images of celebrities sprinkled around social media like confetti. Every New Year weight loss plans and diets are advertised on our screens, closely followed by their summer ready bikini body counterparts. We live within diet culture: fawn all over it, criticise it, worship it. Everything is about weight. We are all too light or too heavy, too thin or too fat.

Instead of fixating on Body Mass Index and colourful boxes which may or may not indicate someone's level of health, we need to be more individual; look at physical health on an individual basis, make the time to assess someone's wellbeing in its entirety and take into account the history that an individual has with their relationship with their body and the food they use to fuel it.

We cannot continue to live in a world where the advice to someone who has lived with an eating disorder their entire adult life is to just give in to it.

Never too much and always enough

Cara Lisette

CW: Restrictive eating behaviours, disordered eating

I have always wondered what it must be like to feel at home in your body, to feel as though it's the right 'fit' for you, to feel a connection to it.

For as far back as I can remember, I have oscillated on a spectrum between disconnection from my body to total distain for it. The overwhelming feeling of taking up more space than I deserve to has followed me from my childhood to now, where I exist as a woman in my thirties still coming to terms with the fact that my body will never be small enough for me to feel deserving of the space I occupy.

At seven years old I scrutinised each holiday polaroid, comparing myself to the other children standing in their swimming costumes around the pool. At nine I sat on my living room floor, spinning around a cardboard Weight Watchers wheel and learning for the very first time which foods were 'good' and which were 'bad'. At eleven I cried in the school uniform shop changing rooms, my stomach and thighs red raw from my nails scraping against my skin as I grabbed it over and again, wishing I could pull every gram of fat off my body. By thirteen, I was anorexic.

I wish I could go back to my younger self and tell her those feelings of wanting to disappear would pass, and that with age she would realise there were more important things in life than her weight. I wish I could say something that would make her believe she was worth more than the space she took up, and to tell her to channel her determination, perfectionism and fierce independence in the right direction, lest they end up being her downfall. I wish I could tell her that she could achieve so much more with these characteristics than starving herself. But instead, I can only mourn for the experiences lost to my eating disorder, and vow to not allow it to take any more years from me.

Being diagnosed with an eating disorder at such a young age meant my identity was formed around it very quickly. I wasn't just Cara, I was Cara with anorexia. I was Cara who threw away her snacks and spent her school lunch money on cigarettes. I was Cara who missed lessons to go to therapy, and ultimately, I was Cara who left education altogether and went to an inpatient facility, where I stayed for the next six months.

During my time in hospital, I relearnt how to eat 'normally'. I also learnt how to lie about how much I was eating, how to purge without anybody noticing, and how to exercise in secret. I came out of hospital heavier than I went in, but my anorexic brain remained very present in my life and my thoughts about myself and my body remained unchanged. I left feeling like I was living in somebody else's body; it was as though I was wearing a skin-suit that was too big for me. I didn't recognise myself in the mirror. I wish I could tie my recovery story up in a little bow after I was discharged back into the community, but sadly it wasn't to be.

Every relapse I had subsequently felt worse than the one before. Each time I fell harder and faster. My entire twenties were consumed by a series of vengeful re-emergences of my eating disorder, and eventually days turned to months turned to years. I would exist with anorexia until I couldn't tolerate it anymore and ask for help from the eating disorders service. I'd have a course of therapy to get me back into a more stable place, and then a couple of years later succumb to it again: my own Groundhog Day.

Every morning when I was unwell I would wake up and immediately feel panic wash over me: Did I really eat that or was it a dream? What did I eat yesterday? Have I lost weight? I'd lay in bed tapping my hip bones to see if they felt more prominent than the day before. I would get up to weigh myself, joints aching as I stepped on and off the scales over and over and again, willing them down just a little more. Then it was time to stand in front of the mirror and examine my body from every conceivable angle. The rush of adrenaline from seeing my weight drop would always disappear as quickly as it arrived and then I would be instantly filled with dread about having to survive another day of avoiding food; the one thing I couldn't stop thinking about. I would try to go about my day but concentrating on anything felt impossible. I couldn't hold conversations or read or watch the television. The only thing that could hold my attention was the thousands of recipes and photographs of food I scrolled through for hours on end, all the while taunted by a voice narrating my every waking minute: 'fat fat fat fat fat fat fat fat'. Every single person I saw became my competition: Do I eat less than them? Are they thinner than me? My arms and thighs were always pink from grabbing at them all day, checking to see if they had doubled in size every time food passed my lips. I would go to bed and lay wide awake, mentally adding up everything I'd eaten while suffocating in guilt and anxiety. Then I would wake up the next day and do it all again.

And that's how I existed, on and off, for large chunks of my adulthood.

I haven't been somebody who has been consistently unwell. Therapy no doubt helped me to have long periods of stability, during which I was able to achieve a degree and a career as a nurse, have a long-term relationship and start a small business. I have been fortunate enough to travel, to go to festivals, to build memories with friends and family that will last a lifetime. I have written a book, continued into postgraduate education and excelled in public speaking. But all the while, I never managed to shake that feeling of disgust at my body. I could never switch off the calorie counter. The anorexic voice, though quieter at times, never went away, and each time it came back it was louder.

I tricked myself into thinking I could function with anorexia forever, but as time passed and I got older I realised this wasn't true. Eventually, after yet another relapse, my job was on the line. My relationships were strained and my holidays were cancelled. My physical and mental health were plummeting and eventually came the time where I had to admit defeat and decide to say goodbye to my eating disorder once and for all. I wasn't a kid anymore; I had responsibilities and a life that I'd worked hard to build. I took an enforced six months off work and entered a day patient service, the most intensive support I'd had since my hospital admission fourteen years earlier. I let my meals be controlled by professionals; I opened up in therapy more than I ever had before; and I dedicated myself to recovery in a way I'd never truly committed to it in the past.

Since I have thrown myself into recovery so entirely, I have felt like I am having to learn who I am again. I have set myself new goals that are completely separate from my eating disorder, and that don't revolve around weight loss and step counts. I have gradually been able to turn down my anorexic voice and I have come to terms with the fact that it may never be truly silent, but that I am strong enough to manage it regardless. I am no longer Cara the anorexic, who throws away her snacks and spends her school lunch money on cigarettes. I'm not just Cara who went to hospital, who attended day patient, who disappeared from work for six months. I'm learning that I am more than that.

I have explored the world solo, I've got a degree and a job I dreamt of. I have won awards for my studies, my work and my writing. These are all things to be *so* proud of and are a part of who I am. But something I have learnt in therapy this time around is that not all achievements are tangible. Not everything requires a trophy or a certificate or a numerical value to be of importance, and many things in my life that mean the most to me don't belong on a CV. They are my relationships with others, the enjoyment I get from my hobbies and my ability to help people. Equally, the qualities people value in me are not my accolades or my weight, but my kindness, sense of humour and intelligence.

It was not easy to get to this point. I always believed recovery was for other people, but not for me. It was too late for me. I've been ill for too long. Maybe they could do it but I can't, because I'm different. There have been years and years of torture in treatment: standing in my underwear on the scales in the hospital, forcing down litre upon litre of milk in day treatment, pushing myself to sit and rest when I wanted nothing more than to walk and walk all day. Hours and hours of therapy have been completed over many months and years and decades. Today, I know myself better than I ever have. I am a chronic perfectionist and I constantly feel like I need to be in control. I struggle with the idea that I have no value as a person unless I am achieving things, and I have, up until now, always considered my ability to starve myself as my biggest achievement.

But now, for the first time, it feels like I can build an identity for myself outside of my eating disorder. Yes, I have struggled with anorexia, and yes it has been there on and off for most of my life. But I am also ambitious and smart and creative. I love cats and pyjamas and sitcoms. I am passionate about equal rights and using my experiences to help others. Most importantly, I have been able to find happiness again, outside the prison of my eating disorder. I can be fully present when I'm with the people I love. I can watch films and read books. I can sleep through the night and wake up feeling at peace. Now, I can go for walks and count the flowers I see, not the steps I have taken.

So, to my body now, I say this: I am sorry. Despite the years I tortured you with starving and purging and exercising to the point of collapse, you somehow kept me alive. You have continued to exist against all odds, and you have never given up on me regardless of how much I sometimes wished you would. For so many years I went to bed with chest pain and anxiety, fearing I might not wake up the next day, yet every morning you were there, helping me to face another day battling against my mind. For everything I put you through, I am sorry. I do not love you yet, and most of the time I barely even like you. But slowly, I am learning to appreciate you.

It is true that, through recovery, my body is bigger today. But so is my life.

And I am finally starting to believe that I deserve the space I take up.

Every last bit of it.

Towards a Kingless Kingdom

Clare Fisher

cw. Restrictive eating behaviours,
exercise addiction, gender dysphoria

'Illness is the night side of life, a more onerous
citizenship. Everyone who is born holds dual citizenship,
in the kingdom of the well and in the kingdom of the
sick. Although we all prefer to use the good passport,
sooner or later each of us is obliged, at least for a spell,
to identify ourselves as citizens of that other place.'

Susan Sontag, Illness as Metaphor (1978)

You, women would, way back in that other world – the *before* of the end of my thirteen-year relationship, the Tory landslide, the Australian wildfires, the pandemic – tell me, *are so tiny! So healthy!* By this they meant: you run, you eat vegetables, you're able-bodied, you're thin. If such comments were accompanied by diet talk, or a comment about how my 'high metabolism' wouldn't last forever, I might, if I was feeling brave, say that I'd struggled with food as a teenager but that I'm fine now. I'd pronounce the 'ed' clearly, before shunting the conversation as far away from my body as possible. I did not want anyone to hear the words 'well' and 'woman' clashing awkwardly against my skeleton, like stolen goods I'd stashed in my underpants.

The first lockdown compounded my citizenship confusion. As a young, able-bodied, single, childless person whose income as a PhD researcher and lecturer was unaffected by the pandemic, I was in an extremely privileged position – relative to many of my friends, and to the people I encountered on my daily doom scrolling. A few months in and I could barely remember what it was like to have a cold, a stomach bug, an unexplained injury, a hangover; to arrive in a physical classroom sweaty and pissed off from a commute, rather than groggy from sleep. If wanted to run, I could run. If I wanted to eat mostly vegetables for dinner, no one would stop me. If I was bored of my Zoom call, I could nod whilst scrolling through the Instagram pages of the trans guys and nonbinary afab people whose feelings about gender and body were remarkably similar to mine (not that I could be trans or nonbinary because the stolen goods I often felt my womanhood to be – a stolen hood, perhaps? – was just a metaphor, a bad one, and metaphors weren't real). Health, I thought, was being productive all the time. 'Well' was being in complete control.

Come summer 2020 and I was, like millions of other clinically 'well' people in the UK, drinking many beers in many parks. Occasionally I'd drink enough to blurt out that when I looked in the mirror and saw a body that looked like a woman's, it felt fundamentally wrong, that this was another reason I maintained what I'd only recently admitted was a 'problematic' relationship to food and exercise. I'd be sure, however, to hedge any claims with copious quantities of 'maybes' and 'I don't knows' and 'nothings.'

I was going to write that I was also, at this time, eating many crisps, but then I replaced *many* with *some*, before replacing some with this sentence, and even so, I cannot convey how that *some* made my heart thump like I'd committed a heinous crime. Nor would such a sentence show at what proportion of these meet-ups I was too dizzy or hangry or sad or numb or preoccupied with calculating how I'd 'burn off' said crisps – thank *god* I could now leave the house multiple times a day – to engage fully.

Occasionally, a window would open – I was going to write, 'as if from nowhere', but in truth, it was usually when a friend or a partner called me out on some behaviour or another. We'd talk, and I'd see that they could see that maybe the room I thought I'd been in, of my own volition, was a cage. They were outside, in what looked like fresh air, and if I got help, maybe I could climb out there, too. It was in such a mood that I finally booked an appointment with the doctor. His words – 'You're underweight but not dangerously so; it's just a phase…' – echoed that of the voice that I was still sure had nothing to do with anorexia: 'What are you complaining about? You eat all the time, you greedy pig.'

#

Over the second and third lockdowns, the voice got LOUD. It would bark me awake at 6:00 am every morning, and thus would begin the relentless cycle of running, working, walking, eating as little as possible, which was always more than 'it' wanted. It was difficult to imagine how I might get past the series of internal customs officers who'd let me back into the kingdom in which you could moan about not being bothered to go for a run, then tuck into a huge piece of cake. I was constantly cold, rarely slept, grew downy hair on my face. I alternated between barely finding the energy to climb the two sets of stairs to the room in which I worked, slept, did HIIT workouts, Zoomed friends, cried, watched Netflix, let alone think all the 'clever' things I was for some insane reason being paid to try and write for my PhD, and being unable to sit still, so full was I with a zingy, springy energy. 'I'm like a teenage boy on speed,' I'd joke. Then, one friend told me she found it 'painful' how my body now look liked a boy's. Still, I didn't say: 'But that's what I wanted all along.' The weird thing was that by the time I was finally diagnosed as belonging to the 'sick', and by a doctor who shook her head sadly at my earlier encounter with her (now retired, male) colleague, I felt much closer to 'well' than I had for a long time. The teenage joyrider must've been in the ascendant that day, I guess.

#

Words aren't real and neither is much of what 'happens' in our minds but our bodies are, and we have to live in them, no matter what. In the months since lockdown has (for now, at least) ended, I've started to come out as neither properly belonging to the kingdom of the well or of women. I'm nonbinary. I have anorexia. I've said it online. I've said it IRL. The more I say it, the more I can hear that anorexia's voice is not my own. I would like to say that I'm writing this with my feet on firmly healthful ground, but I can't, not yet.

What I can, however, say, is that I am turning away from the Customs Officials. I am ripping up my passport and trying, with the help of friends, comrades, and the help I've been lucky to finally receive from the NHS, to make a new one. So many 'recovery narratives' are predicated upon gaining weight so you can run marathons, achieve at work, get married... And while I will not rule out doing any of these things, what I want, right now, is to live in a kingdom whose citizenship is not contingent on me *being* a certain way, *doing* a certain thing or *achieving* a certain outcome; a kingless kingdom.

To live there, you do not have to show a passport, or pour your body into a shape that will communicate all the pain and the joy and the weirdness of your relationship to it, because bodies aren't metaphors, they are just bodies, and to be a person in a body in the kingless kingdom, you only have to live. There is a Universal Basic Income, which is care. I'm not there yet, no way, but where I am is a place where I don't even care that I've not run for months. When I can book an exercise class then cancel it because I'm too tired or just because I don't feel like it. When I can go out for a meal with friends and, when the voice comes for me, I can tell them, and they can say, it's not real, and I can almost see how absurd I must look from their perspective. And while it doesn't *feel* like I'm getting better, I do, every once in a while, feel a breezy sort of silence, and then I turn around, and there, right behind, I mean, inside me of me, is a window, and it's wide, wide open, and one of these days, I'll find the courage to climb out.

The Gadget

Ade Couper

A couple of months ago I ended up buying a gadget. It was one of those things to help with opening bottles, jars, and the like, that you often see advertised on Facebook, or in those supplements you find shoved into a copy of the *Radio Times*. 'So what?' you might think. Maybe I'm elderly, or I have arthritis or something similar. That's true. Not the elderly bit. But I do have a condition that impacts on my abilities to do some of those things that the rest of the population perhaps takes for granted. Still, why am I telling you this story?

Let's wind the clock back to early 2017. I'm an ordinary bloke, late middle-aged, living alone, working, and basically just getting on with life. When suddenly I'm hit with a diagnosis: Primary Progressive Multiple Sclerosis, or MS for short. It's fair to say it knocked me back, and I think it took me the best part of 18 months to get my head around it.

It's not as though I hadn't had health issues before: I had been diagnosed with type 2 diabetes in 2007 and had a heart attack in 2015. So, what was the difference here? I think it was predominantly due to me having some control over the diabetes and the heart condition: living a healthier lifestyle; eating properly; taking some regular exercise. They weren't going to make health problems go away, but doing those things gave me an element of control. Basically, if things went tits up with either of the above problems, it was likely due to me not watching my lifestyle. Whereas the MS, that wasn't something I could control with diet or lifestyle. In fact, that was going to get worse no matter what I did. The clue is in the name – Primary Progressive MS – it's going to progress pretty much whatever I do, and therein lies the problem.

If you were to see me, you probably wouldn't take that much notice. 50-something year old bloke, 6ft tall, carrying a bit of extra weight (although not too much), shaved head, beard, and using a walking stick. Nothing there to make you think I'm disabled necessarily. However, when I look in the mirror, I see a cripple looking back. I see the wreck of a human body, not someone who would 'pass' as able-bodied. Effectively, I have a form of body dysmorphia.

This is a hurdle I can't get over. Objectively I understand that people who don't know me well likely wouldn't see me as disabled. But I cannot square that with how I see (or maybe a more accurate term is visualise) myself – and that causes some major issues for me.

I'm not entirely sure what caused this, but I can think of a few things that have contributed. This includes abuse from people. It's not unheard of for me to be standing at a bus stop, minding my own business, only for the peace to be shattered by someone shouting… well, I'm sure you can fill in that blank. And does anyone else intervene? Now, I can give as good as I get when it comes to people shouting abuse at me, but I'll be honest, it does get you down. I've thought about reporting this to the Police, as it is technically a hate crime, but unless they've got CCTV and audio… and I really don't know if I could deal with it if it did end up going to court.

I think another factor has been how some in my extended family have reacted to my diagnosis. There are some who have basically said that this is my own fault, and some who have even implied this illness is a kind of judgement on me. Again, you try to ignore things like that, or laugh them off, but it does prey on your mind.

I actually think what I'm saying here, which I've only said to a few trusted friends, may well surprise people. Since I got over the news of the diagnosis (and it did take between 12 and 18 months to process) my attitude has been, I think, very positive. I've acknowledged that I have a life-long condition that is going to adversely affect (and ultimately shorten) my life, but I refuse to let it rule me, and I carry on as best I can for as long as I can. Although I have been aware of my dysmorphia (for want of a better term) for quite a time now, this is the first time I've really articulated how it makes me feel…

If I were to try to sum it up in one word it would be 'dependent'. I know that there are tasks I used to do without a second thought, changing a lightbulb for instance. One of the ways my MS affects me is that my balance is now extremely poor, so I can't just climb a set of steps to change a bulb, I need someone to do it for me. It makes me very conscious of what I can do now versus what I used to be able to do. I used to really enjoy long-distance walking and would often do a walk of between 10 and 20 miles, which isn't going to happen anymore. I'm conscious of these issues with my balance when I'm outside, say walking to the local shop, and worry everyone is looking at me because I'm lurching rather than walking. I think that because I've had a lot of, for want of a better term, bullying, over how I look and the like, I am very self-conscious about how I 'present' to the outside world, and the difficulties I experience due to the MS have only made me more self-conscious. Again, I'm conscious that my perception of things is actually quite different to the reality of the situation, but I cannot see how I can square this particular circle.

So, how do I move forward, and away from this mindset, which is causing me real problems? Counselling and/or therapy is an option, but as someone who works in mental health, I know how long the waiting lists are. I know there are treatments out there for dysmorphia, but my understanding is that they are predominantly geared towards a certain type of body dysmorphia. Whether some form of self-help tools, such as CBT or mindfulness would be helpful, I don't know, but it's something I will be looking into. There are gadgets available for whatever this problem might be. I will one day learn to use them.

Digging for the Bones

Rue Collinge

This is what's left of one human being,
this thing on a slip of gauze

from the Japanese poem 'Revelation', Koichi Kihara, 1922[1]

I miss writing with my hands ELLIPSIS The world has always made sense as soon as I have my notebook COMMA and I miss it with a belly–wrenching INSERT DASH BEFORE WRENCHING END OF LINE COMMA world-turned-sideways INSERT DASH AFTER WORLD INSERT DASH AFTER TURNED END OF LINE kind of hurt FULL STOP There is no other part of my body I would notice missing more than my arms COMMA and now somehow I am on an awkward first date in a long-term relationship INSERT DASH AFTER LONG END OF LINE COMMA and I've forgotten how to do it all FULL STOP

6 September 2017, 8:17 AM

---

[1] Koichi Kihara, *Japanese Poetry Now*, ed. and trans. by Thomas Fitzsimmons (New York: Schocken Books, 1972), p.36

It's 2016. Ask me what a writer looks like. They wear glasses (probably). Their office is a coffee shop, or a room clotted with books, or a tree trunk from which they can watch the world go by.

My understanding of the writer's process was admittedly no better. In my mind, writing was a tangible act of creation. I saw a writer more akin to a potter: unless they had their hands on the raw material, they couldn't shape it. That meant a notebook, or a keyboard; there was no in–between. The process was a mystery that I enjoyed. I *liked* that people envisioned me as some romantic figure, waxing lyrical by candlelight.

Now, I agree with editors such as Crowe and Oltermann who want 'to tear down the invisible wall between us readers and them writers and see what's really going on behind the page',[2] because frankly it isn't a very interesting mystery.

I *do* wear glasses, and I used to frequent my local coffee shop to help me focus – but life now is starkly different. Four years ago, I was diagnosed with a health condition which severely limits the use of my hands and wrists, so I write with my hands in my lap, with a headset, and a computer *bristling* with dictation software. Writer's cramp is no longer the issue; instead, it is the possibility of losing my voice! I can be speaking for up to ten hours a day, depending on the task at hand.

My relationship with this life-changing software has not been an easy one. Dictation is imperfect, but so is the person dictating. After my diagnosis, I struggled to translate what

---

[2] *How I Write: The Secret Lives of Authors*, ed. by Dan Crowe & Philip Oltermann (New York: Rizzoli, 2007), p.4

I was thinking into good content, punctuated as it was with the voice commands necessary to navigation and editing. I couldn't maintain a creative stream with this constant attention to the nuts and bolts.

Words were reduced to building blocks. Vocalising my thoughts was a stilted, unnatural process. Before, I had been able to condense those first flashes of thought into a coherent sentence – with my keyboard or pen. Now, I was frustrated by their disconnected nature. They spilled onto the page and I tried – unsuccessfully – to connect the dots. In my failure to communicate, I stopped trying to innovate. I did only as much as was required to complete my undergraduate degree, but I didn't write outside of it. I was too busy grieving for what I had lost.

By the time I began a Masters degree, I had a better facility with the software, but there was still a yawning chasm between what was in my head and what ended up on the page. I had always hoped 'to hear that there was some magic about writing, and to be initiated into the brotherhood of authors'.[3] Don't we all? Well, it had always felt like magic, but now it felt like hard work. I was digging in the mud, but I was uncovering very little treasure. My enjoyment melted away in the face of this gloomy slogging. I could no longer see a future in which I would be able to write well, and it scared me.

Brande may have been writing in 1934, but her words resonated with me. Why did I still cling to this old fairytale? Why should there be a magical shortcut for writing? I was

---

[3.] Brande, Dorothea, *Becoming a Writer*, (New York: Harcourt, Brace, 1934), p.22

suitably chastened. It was clear that I needed to *train* if I were to better translate my thoughts. My difficulty was that I had yet to perceive dictation as anything more than a crude tool with which I could approximate my old creative process.

As Hall points out, often 'Our minds are musclebound, not by intellect, but by formulas of thought'.[4] I was a prisoner of my own making. Granted, my body no longer worked as expected, but I lived *now*. In any other period of history, this would have ended my career. Instead, I had access to technology that was uniquely suited to my line of work, and with practice I would be able to contend with my peers. I became convinced that I could achieve as much – if not more – with this new technology as with traditional methods. But how?

That same advice appeared wherever I looked: write often, in quantity, and without editing as you go. Brande compares the mechanism of writing to exercise, to which we can become better accustomed as long as we practice.[5] This stamina grows as writing becomes a habit which we cultivate. I was writing a journal at the time, and realised (with a tone of surprise) that:

> It is brilliant and useful to write rubbish. Probably most of this is. Sifting through – mining for the gold – is part of the process. Writing for no one but myself is the goal here. I am not trying to find the shape of

---

[4] Donald Hall, *Writing Well*, 6th edn. (Illinois: Scott, Foresman/Little Brown College Division, 1988) p.19

[5] Dorothea Brande, *Becoming a Writer*, (New York: Harcourt, Brace, 1934), p.71

the finished product. I am not considering my audience.
I am not writing for applause or adulation. I am
writing because in order to get better, I must.[6]

I practised. I couldn't just create nonsense, because the effort of editing it all later was too lengthy. I had to learn to distil it. Dictation has forced me to organise my thoughts differently, to know what I want to say before I speak it aloud. How can I best translate what I'm thinking? Which words will best capture the story I am telling?

I began to see parallels in the challenges of translation, of works from another language. The anthology *Japanese Poetry Now* has been, according to the translator, 'remade into English',[7] not translated. This choice of language is spot-on! The phonetic and logographic differences are huge in contrast to any European language, and when you take cultural aesthetic into account, the task is monumental. As Fitzsimmons approached each poem for the collection, he tussled with how 'to preserve rather than reduce mystery' whilst still trying to reproduce 'with fidelity to pattern and whole, the human vision vibrant there'.[8]

I am determined to remain faithful to the mental catalyst which inspires me, but I am doing so with a brand new language. Through this process, I have developed a greater precision with words. I have also developed a greater appre-

---

[6]. *Process Creative Journal*, 16/10/2018, Appendices p.2
[7]. *Japanese Poetry Now*, ed. and trans. by Thomas Fitzsimmons (New York: Schocken Books, 1972), p.iii
[8]. *Japanese Poetry Now*, ed. and trans. by Thomas Fitzsimmons (New York: Schocken Books, 1972), pp.11-12

ciation for the relationship between form and content, especially in poetry. As formatting my work must be achieved by voice commands, detail needs to be worth the time expenditure. A poet is less distracted by form for form's sake – or gimmicky concrete aspirations – when it is painstakingly achieved. This new understanding (and long hours of practice) have allowed me to develop a writing process which is far more robust than it ever was.

In this process of digging, I have found I am excavating self, piece by piece. I am coal-smudged, dirty – grinning with new callouses on my hands from this work mining words. Not all my forays are successful or productive. I don't bring back gold with every trip, and I still groan from the strain and shrink from the labour, but I am learning the tunnels and trying new parts of the rock face.

I am mining for gold. See – how it gleams in the dirt.

* A significantly different version of this essay was previously published online at *Fragmented Voices*.

My Body, My Captor

Abbie Rutherford

After years of wrangling with the imprisonment of you, my body, and the Myalgic Encephalomyelitis you harbour within, I believed I had gained control over you and finally mastered how to prevent you from returning to your role as governor; warden; oppressor.

For a sustained period of time, I had seen you in a more positive light. We appeared to reach an agreement within our dysfunctional relationship. I continued to take my medication and lead a more muted existence than before, while you gave me some respite and dulled the symptoms. That existence had been happier; I had achieved things I would never have felt were possible before you allowed the illness to lodge in us, and the first tentacles of an uneasy alliance were formed. You no longer felt like the enemy, and we co-existed quietly, calmly, and without the drama of the previous ten years.

Don't get me wrong, you have always been there to remind me of your potential power: the dizziness on a warm day as I try to enjoy a weekend of activities; the gnawing pain you would produce when I overstepped the mark in a physical pursuit; the fatigue in its various manifestations, from bearable to dragging myself around. But we have rubbed along together quite nicely. That symbiotic relationship between myself as the psychological me and you the physical me, with all your quirks and unfathomable (even to the medical professionals) ways and habits, felt natural as we slipped into our own personal 'new normal'.

No longer living a life confined both within your inner walls and the outer walls of the bedroom, I was able to function, to achieve, and build something that was happy and more than just tolerable. It felt as though you were, finally, cooperating with me and that we had started to join forces against the M.E.; rather than battling separately, with you on the side of the coloniser and me, the colonised. You were giving me a break and appeared to remember that we were the joint force; not you and the chronic illness. The complete and total upheaval that you put me through during your rebellious phase began to have an alternative purpose: you forced me into making the changes I needed to make in my life.

Yes, I started to feel grateful towards you and, in a strange way, thankful that you had put me through this.

Subsequently, as Covid-19 spread across the globe and we went into lockdown in March 2020, I felt that I could cope with the situation better than most. After all, I had spent a number of years in my own personal lockdown when you, my body, sided with M.E. and completely consumed me. Although fearful of the virus and the impact it would have on us, you, the malfunctioning body I had despised, had trained me for this. In a way, you had forced me to set my life up for this experience, almost as though you knew: my body as Nostradamus. We had returned to being a team of equals and were perfectly able to cope with the pandemic and its restrictions. In some ways I felt smug; while people around me struggled with their insular lives, together we thrived.

Of course, this couldn't last. It wasn't long before I was reminded that you treated me differently to how other bodies treat their people, and that our normal could never be everyone's normal. Now restrictions have lifted, you once again have me caught, Hotel California-esque, within the confines of our home. Fear of how Covid-19 could take us back to the place we were ten years ago has turned you into my captor, again, by proxy.

I look enviously on as those with cooperative bodies resume their lives. I long to be able to partake in that carefree and blasé mindset that normally functioning people seem to have regained. You have, once again, turned against me but in a more abstract way. I doubt you and your ability to come out of the virus unscathed if we catch it. Simultaneously, I doubt my emotional and psychological self for not resuming life to the fullest we can in the way the majority seem to be doing. It's almost as though I am being gaslighted by my own flesh and bones.

The old bitterness I felt towards you has returned, only this time it feels more significant; almost overbearing. The work I have put in to getting you where we are today feels wasted, and I continue to take the medications without any real recompense. It's irrational, I know, to place the blame on you – you had no control over the pandemic – but while I feel well, I am still imprisoned by the 'what if' you have imposed on me.

However, I know that it is me that needs to resolve this negativity, to reach out an olive branch to you, my body, and accept that this time you are not the enemy.

So, we wait – and wait. I wait for the psychological strength and courage to take a risk and see what the implications may be. I wait to appreciate you again as I try to hold on to the acknowledgement of how far we have come together. I wait to regain the respect I had towards you. And we both wait, together, for an ending; a time when we can once again live harmoniously, with all your quirks and flaws, and without fear as a unit that – for better or worse – we ultimately are.

An authentic portrait of my family's meals

Clare Law

I once had to edit a guide to cafés for a publisher whose business model precluded paying for professional images. The café owners, who had paid to be in the guide, submitted pictures that resembled plates of vomit and I felt sick myself at using them. Food photography is difficult. You need know what food is photogenic and you need to know how to garnish it, arrange it and light it. Then you need to know how to photograph it. That's why 'food stylist' and 'food photographer' are career choices.

I don't tend to share our meals on social media because 'food styling' and 'photography' are not skillsets I have chosen to develop. But the plate of noodle soup I am about to serve to my children, I would like to share on social media. I am proud of this pretty meal. It is leftovers to avoid waste: chicken meat (organic) with soup made from the bones. I have made it nutritious and appealing with bright, fresh, ethically-sourced vegetables shredded, sliced and cross-chopped.

This camera-friendliness was not my intention. I did it not for visual effect but so that my children would not sort through their supper and leave a tidemark of rejected food round the rim of their dishes.

My children's plates are an identity badge and a virtue signal. This is what we – who try to be decent people following the advice of dietary experts and leaders in virtue – eat. And as a parent, I am efficient and effective: I don't cook separate meals because we eat together, all the same food.

#

As the pandemic recession bit harder a few of the mums at school shared a post on Facebook about bringing a discreet bag of shopping to anyone having a hard time: 'No questions asked, no explanation needed'. Everyone commented how kind they were.

I, too, was struck by the plight of the 'quietly desperate'. I knew they were out there – families on a suddenly reduced income who still believed themselves to be people who give to a foodbank, not people who receive from it.

I wanted to help.

I offered each weekend takeaway boxes of whatever family meal I was cooking: lentil chili, chickpea stew, sausage casserole. Each week five or ten people commented on the post or at the school gates saying how kind I was. 'What a lovely thing to do!' I enjoyed the approval.

Then they asked me, by direct message or when we were alone, if I'd had any takers. They wondered if they should be offering the same.

There were no takers.

'That must be disappointing,' someone said across the two-metre pandemic gap.

I didn't admit that I had no idea what I would do if someone said, 'Yes please.' A meal cannot save a family in crisis. It makes a difference for a single afternoon – and then what? Once you know a family is in trouble, is the etiquette that you keep sending casserole until they ask you to stop?

I also didn't admit that I wondered if the quietly desperate people were disgusted by me or by my kitchen, or by my idea of a healthy, wholesome family meal. Or perhaps they saw me as nosey, fishing for information.

I stuffed these doubts alongside the unwanted boxes of food in the back of the freezer.

I replied that it wasn't about the food and feeding of people. 'It's a message: everyone wants you to have food, so you shouldn't be ashamed to get your needs met.'

I opened the offer to anyone too tired and stressed to cook. 'No questions asked,' I reminded them. 'Smaller portions available,' I said to welcome quietly desperate singletons.

I started to feel brittle as I made my offerings, as if someone might tell me off for fake virtue. But I couldn't stop: I imagined a quietly desperate, tired or stressed person screwing up their courage to say, 'Yes please.'

Then one week I spent Sunday afternoon roasting a piece of belly pork until the meat slipped from the bones and parted from the silky fat and rust-coloured crackling. The meat was delicious. The meal was good humoured and cheerful and I was so proud of my work. I did not offer any of the pork because we wanted it for ourselves cold the next day. Also it seemed insulting to give pieces from a roast dinner, like offering scraps. And I feared the judgement – the sad-face and angry-face reactions – that would ask me to again process the suffering our existence causes and assess – again – the nutritional and ethical values of unfamiliar plant-based foods.

Another week, I was so tired that I refused to cook. We ate food – already offered up to the 'quietly desperate' and perhaps rejected by them – from our freezer.

As the levels of covid-19 went up again, offering boxes of food seemed irresponsible. So I stopped. The quietly desperate people would have to put aside their reservations and go through official, covid-safe channels. Instead, we donated online to the foodbank. But it seemed like showing off to mention that on social media, even though the foodbank would appreciate us normalising giving behaviour.

#

As a child I was a greedy, urgent reader of Laura Ingalls Wilder's accounts of her 1860s childhood pioneering the American Midwest. Her elevation and exaltation of the mundane and the domestic, of a woman's narrative, opened doors as I developed my own writer's voice. But reading the books again to my own children, I see shadows, and not only in her careless, exploitative accounts of non-white people.

My favourite is *On the Banks of Plum Creek*. It's the story of Laura's family – the gentle, practical, pious Ma; the hardworking but restless Pa; saintly sister Mary; and wilful but mostly good Laura – settling yet another piece of land. As a child reader, it seemed idyllic: Laura and Mary playing in a pristine landscape and helping their parents grow, forage or raise what they needed.

The picture on the cover of my now brittle paperback shows Laura and Pa setting a fish trap. The scene in my memory is of a girl and her dad doing pleasant work to feed the family. But now I read that they were in real trouble. They'd spent all their money buying land and putting up a house. Their wheat and vegetables were still growing and fish was all they had – for breakfast, lunch and dinner – for weeks on end. Did Ma and Pa feel badly about their choices? Ingalls Wilder never mentions it.

These books are not simple accounts. Ingalls Wilder wrote

them as a middle-aged wife and mother. The portraits of her at this time resemble my grandmothers in their dress and manner. It is difficult to square them with the images of Laura and Mary paddling in Plum Creek: her childhood seems to come from a different age to her adulthood. Ingalls Wilder and her daughter Rose Wilder Lane chopped and diced the narrative until it signalled an ideal of fierce and proud independence, a belief in providence and the choice to live in a place where the land would give and give and give.

#

If I could take good food portraits, this is what I would share about our family meals: our children enjoy these worthy, wholesome foods; we buy local; we buy organic; we have plenty but we do not waste.

And I think about what actually happens at our family meals. I place a 'healthy plate' in front of each child: half vegetables, one quarter carbs and one quarter protein. Then my children unbalance my calibrated meals. They gobble up the carbs and leave the protein then try to claim what is on our plates. One identifies as vegetarian and cries at the sight of bones but then rejects veggie burgers and bean dishes. The other gags on plant-based protein, whines that her meat contains no bones to gnaw and sorts vegetables into cold heaps on the side of her plate. Several times a week someone storms from the table and I can't in honesty say it's never been me.

The anxiety about their health in later life, their teeth, their bones, their gut flora, their hormones, their stress levels is so overwhelming that I must shut it down to get us safely through a meal. I buy organic and follow only the most basic of nutritional advice. Anything else is more than I can bear. I can't bring myself to learn about paleo, veganism, omega oils and cortisol from videos shared by better mummies than me.

My desired picture does not hold up. Those photos resembling plates of sick, the result of anxiety-induced nausea, would be the most honest portrait of my food experience.

Tangled

Val Fraser

There's chocolate in the room, just over there.

Two metres away. Seven steps away. Twelve seconds away. A coffee table and two bits of flattened carpet away.

A blue-jeaned leg blocks my view, hiding the shiny purple wrapper. I could get up out of my seat and walk over there, across the first bit of carpet, around the coffee table, across the second bit of carpet, around the blue-jeaned leg right to where the chocolate is.

There's chocolate in the room, but it isn't mine. It belongs to someone else. I ate my share of chocolate yesterday. And now it's gone. All gone. Not a bite left. I am without chocolate, but there is chocolate in the room.

I could ask the blue jeaned owner of the chocolate to share it with me. I could open my mouth and speak. I could ask for some; a piece, a chunk. But I don't want a piece or chunk, I want it all. I want all the chocolate in the room. And the primary reason I want all the chocolate in the room is because it is in the room. In this room. The room in which I am also in.

From where I am sitting I cannot see the chocolate, or even the wrapper. I cannot smell the chocolate. I cannot touch the chocolate. I cannot taste the chocolate. I cannot hear the chocolate. None of my five senses can detect the chocolate. But I passed it on my way into the room. My mind logged its exact location and size. The blue jeaned owner is wearing headphones and listening to music. He does not hear the chocolate calling, which I find odd because it's right next to him.

But I can hear the chocolate calling – all the louder because I had chocolate yesterday – saying, 'I am in the room.' There is chocolate *in* the room.

The blue jeaned leg moves. The chocolate in the room is suddenly in my sightlines. A subtly rounded purple edge protrudes above a tumbled stack of books and magazines. A slender strip of lilac light beckons me.

The leg moves back to hide the chocolate. I put the kettle on.

#

Mum wouldn't buy Easter eggs. The reason? They were too expensive. It was deemed to be a colossal rip-off and far more cost effective to buy me a quarter pound bag of dolly mixtures. Years later I'm able to identify the feelings and questions generated by that disappointment. All my friends received a stash of Easter eggs, why was I different? The sense of poverty, powerlessness and deprivation was overwhelming and internal voices convinced me I 'wasn't worth it'. I remember marvelling at a wonderful array of Easter eggs displayed in a shop window and longing, with some considerable force, to have my very own. Childish emotions can be disproportionately intense and consuming, can't they?

Then, one wonderful day, a kindly aunt gave me an Easter egg. The experience of unwrapping and discovering, seductively employs the mind and hands of the ancient gatherer. Not unlike the young lab monkeys who go through the self-constructed ritual of re-wrapping an already peeled banana by placing it back inside its skin, then hiding it, then searching for it, then finding it, then 'peeling' it, before eventually consuming it. On a primal level the whole thrilling tactile Easter egg process was burned into my memory.

So it begins: Carefully un-puzzling the complex flaps of the box without tearing the cardboard; lifting the wrapped egg out; noticing it was considerably smaller than the outer box; searching for an edge to the delicate crinkly foil; peeling back the wispy, fragile hem and glimpsing the patterned surface. Inhaling rich promises through innocent nostrils. Filling tiny palms with golden weight. Breaking open the egg. Squealing at the bag of smarties. Finger-tipping the glossy interior. Snapping the shell apart. And then pop! Pure bliss. Exquisite, piercing bliss.

But fake bliss. This wasn't the emotional high generated by deep happiness, meaning or connection, but it was the next best thing to me. I experienced what I now understand to be the artificially constructed 'bliss factor'. Food manufacturers have gone to great lengths to research the precise combination of sugar and fat which stimulates the sensation of intense pleasure in the human brain.

My young mind was blown. On some deep level I awarded Easter eggs holy grail status. Those eggs became the absolute certain, yet maddeningly unattainable, source of ultimate happiness. Even as a young adult, with a little money in my pocket and the option to buy one, I attributed them with a power they never should have been given. For many lonely years I think, on some level, I kept on waiting and hoping for my next Easter egg to arrive. Like a fairy tale princess, I lay sleeping in my tower secretly wishing that some fellow human would understand me deeply and sense my secret, unresolved longing. They would prove their love by bestowing this most treasured gift upon me in a grand gesture.

#

How did love and chocolate get so tangled up together? How was my heart so easily tricked into believing that a combination of cow's milk, refined sugar, cocoa butter, cocoa mass, vegetable fats, emulsifier and flavourings could replace the warmth of human love from a parent, a romantic partner, a child, or friend? How did that outrageous lie take root? When did it become ok for me to pacify myself with chocolate? I'm weeping now as I ask myself at what point did my love-starved heart accept that paltry substitute?

Who knew that Easter eggs are a master stroke of food manufacturing combined with marketing genius? They masquerade as a representation of the Easter promise of new life. Spring is just around the corner, winter is behind us, sunshine and abundant life are on their way. Each February bright boxes fill the supermarket shelves, rows of pregnant foiled bellies protruding through their oval cardboard windows. Within the hollow box, a hollow egg, and a hollow promise: of winning the secret hidden prize; of receiving; of being filled.

I'm so sorry, Mum. You were right. Easter eggs are a colossal rip-off.

From the Belly

Andrew McMillan

CW: Restrictive eating behaviours,
disordered eating, exercise addiction

Like an outfit that always somehow manages to feel imperfect, I have begun this piece too many times. There is no beginning to return to, only a constant middle, a centre.

Early on in our time together, when my therapist asks me where in the body I feel my anxiety, my answer surprises me. I always imagined that I would say my shoulders; feeling the day's worry in their rigidity, in their tensing. Instead, I say, 'my Belly.' I say I feel the anxiety swilling around in there like when I try to move after drinking too much tea.

No beginning to return to. It has always been there.

I remember sitting on the toilet in the bathroom at my house when I was a child, crying. I remember my mum saying she'd have to go into school, that we couldn't go on like this. I suppose another kid must have said something to me, but I don't remember what it was.

At some point I let my size become my defence; perhaps thinking if I was bullied for my size then I wasn't being bullied for being gay – perhaps it meant people wouldn't notice.

When I was in Year 10 I got flu and was in bed for over a week, barely able to eat. When I went back to school, I'd inevitably lost a little bit of weight. Someone told me I looked good. It was the first time that anyone had ever said that to me – it lodged itself in my brain. A switch got flicked.

Maybe it's not true to say that there is no beginning to return to, perhaps it's that there are too many.

Not being able to fit in trousers that weren't elasticated at primary school/ a teacher making jokes about me being a whale as I undressed for PE/ comments on how much I ate/ on what I ate/ on how I looked better when I didn't/ the constant fear of being the wedge of stomach shown on the TV news when there was a story about obesity/ male fashion models who were getting skinnier and skinnier/ the advert about a belly chasing an inactive man down the street in order to sell sportswear screaming '*belly's gonna get ya*'/ the scream that followed me into the playground/ followed me home/ followed me to the train station where I was meeting a boy for the first time and he looked at my body and told me how his ex boyfriend's stomach hadn't been completely flat/ and how he'd hated that.

Post-flu, a returning. That compliment, still remembered. Knowing the right thing to do is to grow to love the self as it is, to not bend to society's rigid rules of how a body should be.

But too young, too tired of not being wanted. A classmate's compliment is a door and I step through it.

On the other side is a corridor, long, unending. There are photographs on the wall – I recognise myself. Tiny salads in mini Tupperware for lunches. Only ever chewing chocolate. Countless sit-ups a night otherwise something bad might happen to my mum. Trying to outrun my own mind, daily.

I thought if I could shrink my stomach I might shrink myself and become invisible. I wouldn't have to be noticed.

If I wasn't noticed, I might be easier to love.

It's a curious thing to say I was taught something when I

couldn't pinpoint the teacher. But it's something that's all around, like being a biscuit dunked into a hot mug of tea.

I was taught my body was nothing if it wasn't thin or muscular.

I was taught I had nothing to give but my body.

I was told I was nothing. Had nothing.

And it's gonna get ya, it's gonna get ya. It's gonna get ya.

Never Been Quite Right

T.G. Hofman

My body, it's never been quite right. There's nothing inherently wrong with it; it works. But so does my toaster. It doesn't make it a good toaster. It just means it toasts bread. My body is a body in the sense that it works, but that doesn't make it a decent body. It just means it functions. I can walk, talk, breathe, run (not too often), jump (even less often), and it gets me from one place to another. But it's never been quite right.

I've always been just that little bit overweight. Not 'fat' (that horrible, globular word) but cuddly (damning with fake praise). I've yo-yo'd through fads of short-term sure things. I've cut my hair differently to draw attention to the remnants of my cheekbones (they're in there somewhere). I've taken punishment from sadistic gym instructors who seem to think it's, 'All in the mind.' (If it were all in the mind, I'd be a swimwear model by now.) Even at school, I'd dread afternoons in the swimming pool. There were kids there far sturdier than me, but that didn't change how I looked at myself. I would resent my sporty contemporaries for being lithe, athletic paragons of confidence. They smiled more than the rest of us. Their clothes fit more comfortably. Lunch wouldn't cause them pain or shame. I can remember thinking that I had found the causal link between smiling and weight, and decided to see if it worked in reverse. If I smiled more, would I become more athletic? I can tell you for a fact that is not the way it works. Still, it was nice to smile more.

If you met me, you wouldn't know that I struggle. I'm confident, funny, quick-witted (and modest), but behind the facade of well-fed opulence, my structure is constantly under attack. I try my best to give off an air of supreme indifference, sometimes even acceptance of myself and the squidgy, ill-defined edges; the vessel for my brilliant personality. 'Thank god you're funny...' someone once said to me. 'Otherwise, you'd never get laid.' A cruel sentiment just after sex, but a valid point coming from the lingerie model I was sharing my bed with at the time. I suggest that the situation said more about how funny I am than how 'cuddly'.

I laugh off these jokes. I even sometimes make jokes at my own expense. Here, others laugh and I laugh along with them, so they don't feel uncomfortable. But the laughter chips away at the structure, piece by piece; the most damaging laugh being my own. I've even achieved things generally reserved for the fittest of specimens. I've run the London Marathon, for goodness' sake. I very nearly won it as well. If it hadn't been for fourteen thousand people in front of me, being overtaken by the man in the sodding Rhino costume and then having the shame of a chap speed past me with a washing machine strapped to his back. Otherwise it would have been a glorious victory! I would like to take this opportunity to point out that I have won the London Marathon precisely the same number of times a Sir Mo Farah. None. So, I'm not that far from athletic greatness.

Though it is my own fault. I prefer reading to running; I enjoy food over fasting; I opt for wine before water. It's on me. I know it is. I have come to accept that my body image is my own, and I must admit responsibility. I could do better.

That said, people don't like me less because of the few extra pounds. If anything, they probably enjoy my company more.

I'm less threatening or not as self-obsessed. I'm not going to chase after them (unless they have wine or expensive cheese) or challenge them to a duel. They know there will always be seconds for them when I cook and that they are guaranteed three courses as a minimum. As I get older, I know that my body will go from 'not quite right' to 'scrapheap chic'. I'm okay with that. I smile more these days. I have learnt to embrace the food and forget the fasting. Wine is never wasted on me, and if the good Lord intended me to run, they'd have given me a less discerning palate.

I'm okay with 'not quite right'. I wasn't for a long time. But I've learnt to smile more. The dear fellows of swimming pool afternoons are still athletic and lithe, but they're also quantity surveyors. I think I've got the last laugh.

Finding my Skin

Daisy Black

Gingerly, we lowered ourselves in. A tingling, more abrasive than cold, crept across our skin. Entering always takes longer in winter. It means submerging each inch of flesh slowly but steadily, to stop the body going into shock.

'Why do we do this again?' I asked my friend, as my already-numb hands sought to break a path through the ice.

They grinned at me.

'Because all our other hobbies have been cancelled.'

#

I never had to bother about keeping fit before the 2020 lockdown. My hobbies involved dancing several nights a week, while commuter cycling meant fitness was just a side effect of the things I loved.

I'd also never before disliked aspects of my own body. I was happy with my chunky thighs, which carried me across the dance floor and let me take up my full space on train seats. I loved that rowing and lugging bags of grains around a shop in my 20s had given me thick arms that turn into satisfying biceps when I can be bothered to exercise them. I have had hairy legs for over a decade. I thought this comfort in my own skin meant I was a Successful Feminist, somehow immune to the grinding, relentless market forces pushing women to endlessly shape and reshape our bodies.

Turns out that was all bollocks. The pandemic showed me what I'd taken as body confidence was just the fragile insulation of privilege from someone lucky enough to find her chosen exercise fun, easy and pain-free to do.

Cracks started to form when, in the ambitious flush of those early lockdown months, my household started doing daily online yoga videos. 'Yoga with Adriene' had a courageous, cheerful instructor who managed to persuade our bodies into something resembling yoga poses. But while Adriene and I share some things in common – we both happen to be dorky musical theatre geeks – as a petite, very slim woman, she represents female bodily ideals that I don't. Watching and trying to copy the movements of a very different body from my own every day was hard. It made me feel a resentment towards my body I'd not felt before.

Each time I couldn't reach my toes, instead of thinking about the fact my hamstrings were tight from 20 years of sitting at a desk, I looked at my tummy and thought of it as a great lump: an insurmountable evil standing in the way. Looking back at my tensed legs in downward dog gave me an uncomfortably close view of a quivering, cellulite terrain. When we finished Adriene's videos and moved to 'Yoga with Tim' things got a little better, as his body shape is so much more obviously not one I could easily aspire to. I might do all the crescent lunges in the world, but I am never going to become a chirpy skater bro with a triangle for an upper torso.

My other main exercise, the government-permitted daily walk, didn't do much to help either. I love walking but live in Sheffield, which can make even a quick walk round the block a demoralising experience. I can do all the exercise I like, but the fact remains that I grew up in Norfolk and am not built for hills. Even at the fittest times of my life, I still puffed up steep slopes, bright pink and longing for a breather, wheezing like The Little Engine That Couldn't.

#

Things changed when I started open water swimming. That summer, friends and I trudged across a field for a quick, shivering dip in a reservoir, observed by a solemn pack of cows. Under those peaty waters, my skin took on an orange hue, and for the first time in months, felt like my own again.

Wild swimming seems to attract particularly fearless people. Finding watery companions in a group of middle-aged women and nonbinary swimmers, I realised the things I'd started to dislike about my body were also the things helping me swim. As November arrived I got a shorty wetsuit, but even before then the tummy and thighs I'd thought lumpy and ugly were keeping me warm; blubber insulating my core. When I got out, the exposed skin flushed in comic patterns. It's hard to be awkward about your body image while wearing a wetsuit and bobble hat in midwinter, skin bright tomato red in all the places not wrapped in neoprene.

When the February ice crept across the reservoirs, macho men we'd not seen all winter would sometimes join our swim spot. They made a lot of fuss about entering, puffing at the cold, making a big deal of how brave they were. We smiled, snug in our selkie skins, and asked where they'd been during the rain the week before.

When spring came, the reservoirs became more popular. Yorkshire Water sent security guards to stop people swimming, citing hidden depths and the risks of cold water. So far these guards have had limited success when faced with cunning middle-aged women equipped with neoprene socks and tow floats. Aqua trespassers, we've gone way beyond letting others police our bodies and where we choose to put them.

#

When the second lockdown eased, I returned to Norfolk and went swimming in the sea. By now, my body was so used to colder waters a summer dip in the sea felt warm.

As I swam, three seals popped up. The bravest was only a few metres away. It looked at me with vast liquid eyes, and I looked back. Our bodies bobbed, suspended in the water. Buoyant kindred; comfortable in our skin. Then the seal dipped its head, and was gone.

Contributors

Wendy Allen is a poet whose work has appeared in *Poetry Wales*, *Ambit*, *Banshee*, *The Moth* and *Propel*. Her first pamphlet will be published by Broken Sleep in May 2023.

Faye Alexandra Rose is a Pushcart Prize nominated writer and author of three poetry chapbooks: *Incognito* (Bottlecap Press), *Mortal Beings* (Dark Thirty Poetry Publishing), and *Pneuma* (Sunday Mornings at the River) which was shortlisted for a Saboteur Award for Best Poetry Pamphlet. Her first short story collection is due to be published later this year with Querencia Press.

Jaimi Shrive is a director at VictimFocus, and a PhD candidate at King's College London researching the relationship between political ideology and women's access to justice after violent crime.

Kayla Jenkins is a writer currently based in Blackpool. After completing her Creative Writing MA in 2020 at Lancaster University, she published her debut poetry pamphlet *Preservation* in 2022 with Invisible Hands Press. Her writing is inspired by working class lives and the coastal ecosystems surrounding her. She is currently working on her first full-length poetry collection and a novel.

Cassie Evelyn Johnson (she/her) is a writer from Nottingham. She studied law at the University of Bristol and holds a master's degree from the University of Oxford. She now lives in London and is currently finishing her first novel. When distracting herself from that task, she writes short stories and essays. In her other life, she works as a barrister.

Donna M Day is a writer who lives in Liverpool, England. She is a regular theatre reviewer for North West End UK. Her fairy tales appeared in Mother's Milk Books' *The Forgotten and the Fantastical* series, and her poetry appeared in *Key Words: Poems from Lockdown*. Her newsletter 'Sea Invisible' is about life with invisible disability and she is currently blogging her way through Seventy Years of Books.

Cara Lisette is a mental health blogger, author and psychological therapist. She has struggled with her mental health since her childhood, which has mainly centred around eating disorders. In 2015 she was also diagnosed with bipolar disorder, and throughout her twenties has been on a journey to try and learn about herself and focus on her recovery and wellbeing. She spends her days working with children with mental health problems, and outside of this writes and speaks about her experiences with mental illness and how she has learnt to manage this over time. Her main priority is to share her story with the hope that it will help and support others to start their own journeys of self discovery and personal growth.

Clare Fisher is a prose writer and Lecturer in Creative Writing. They are the author of the novel, *All the Good Things* (Viking, 2017), and the short story collections, *How the Light Gets In* (Influx Press, 2018) and *The Moon is Trending* (forthcoming, Salt, 2023). Their work has been published in six territories worldwide, won a Betty Trask Award and been longlisted for the Edgehill Short Story Award and the International Dylan Thomas Prize. They have taught at Goldsmiths College and Queen Mary University London, Leeds University and Leeds Arts University. They live in Leeds.

Ade Couper is a former Worcestershire Poet Laureate, and was born in Bedford in the dim and distant past. Ade works as a mental health link worker, & is an activist for human rights and disability rights. Ade's first poetry collection will be published in 2023 by Black Pear Press.

Rue Collinge is a full-time storyteller and poet in North-East England. Recently she was a semi-finalist for BBC Words First and a UK Online Slam Champion. Raw and lyrical, she has performed across the UK and on the radio. Her day job as a wordtinker finds her equally in festival fields and university halls. She helps people find their voice in an increasingly noisy world.

Abbie Rutherford is a freelance editor and proofreader based in the North East. As someone who consistently says she is not a writer, she is delighted and surprised to find herself in this anthology.

Clare Law is a writer, editor and mother. At threebeautifulthings.co.uk she records on most days three items that pleased or interested her during the previous twenty-four hours. She also writes short fiction and essays. She has a particular interest in narratives that use ephemera and found texts. She edits novels and writes commercial content to support her family. Her creative writing practice supports the skills for which she is paid.

Val Fraser is a trained journalist with over 12 years' experience working on staff in a variety of demanding media environments. She has authored/edited thousands of published articles including news, features and travel. She recently stepped up to the role of Digital Editor with *Sorted Magazine*. @ValFraserUK

Andrew McMillan's debut collection *physical* was the only ever poetry collection to win *The Guardian* First Book Award. The collection also won the Fenton Aldeburgh First Collection Prize, a Somerset Maugham Award (2016), an Eric Gregory Award (2016) and a Northern Writers' award (2014). It was shortlisted the Dylan Thomas Prize, the Costa Poetry Award, *The Sunday Times* Young Writer of the Year 2016, the Forward Prize for Best First Collection, the Roehampton Poetry Prize and the Polari First Book Prize. His second collection, *playtime*, was published by Jonathan Cape in 2018; it was a Poetry Book Society Recommendation for Autumn 2018, a Poetry Book of the Month in both *The Observer* and *The Telegraph*, a Poetry Book of the Year in *The Sunday Times* and won the inaugural Polari Prize. His third collection, *pandemonium*, was published by Jonathan Cape in 2021, and *100 Queer Poems*, the acclaimed anthology he edited with

Mary Jean Chan, was published by Vintage in 2022. He is Professor of Contemporary Writing at the Manchester Writing School at Manchester Metropolitan University and is a fellow of the Royal Society of Literature.

T.G Hofman is a writer based in the Scottish Borders. He has an MA in Creative Writing and has had work produced all over the world. His play, *Shakespeare's Fool*, premiered at the Edinburgh Fringe and subsequently toured the UK before appearing at the National Theatre, Craiova, Romania as part of the International Shakespeare Festival. While his work is mainly in the dramatic form, he enjoys writing narrative short stories and is currently working on his first novel. This is his first published piece of creative non-fiction.

Daisy Black is a medievalist, storyteller and theatre practitioner, and she lectures in English Literature at the University of Wolverhampton. She's published several short stories (most recently with *Hic Dragones*) and has had her plays and stories performed around the UK. Academic publications include a book on gender in early drama with Manchester University Press, and articles on women's performance; the nails used to crucify Christ in medieval pageants; time-travelling trees and medievalism in tabletop gaming. In her spare time she enjoys teaching folk dance and heavy metal morris dancing.

*

Editorial assistance for *From the Body* came from Dione Quirk. Dionne is in her third year of study at the University of Wolverhampton, studying towards an English degree. Her research interests specifically lie within gender studies, queer theory, and narratives of the self. *From the Body* is her first editorial role.

Charley Barnes is an author and academic from the West Midlands, UK. She has taught Creative and Professional Writing at various institutions around the area, including University of Birmingham, University of Worcester, and most recently the University of Wolverhampton. In academia, she specialises in representation in crime fiction, considering the female body and psyche. Alongside this, Charley is currently undergoing research for her first academic monograph, forthcoming with Palgrave MacMillan.

In her poetry and non-fiction, Charley frequently explores representations of and relationships with the body. Her fiction pamphlet, *Your Body is a House Stripped*, is forthcoming with Broken Sleep (2023).